NFTs Explained

How to Create, Buy, Sell, and Use Non-Fungible Tokens for Art, Gaming, and Business

By Joe Correa

Published by Live Stronger Faster

This book is for educational and informational purposes only. The author and publisher are not engaged in rendering legal, financial, or other professional advice. Readers should consult a qualified professional before making any financial decisions.

First Edition

Table of Contents

Introduction

The world changed the moment humans realized that digital items could hold real, verifiable ownership. Not symbolic ownership. Not screenshots. Not files that could be copied infinitely. But ownership that is permanent, traceable, provable, and transferable—just like a deed to a house or the title to a vehicle. This transformation was made possible through a single breakthrough: **the non-fungible token**, the NFT. In Book 3 of the *Metaverse Masterclass* series, we step into one of the most misunderstood yet revolutionary innovations of Web3. This introduction prepares you to see NFTs not as hype, speculation, or internet memes, but as a foundational technology that will power digital identity, creativity, commerce, branding, entertainment, and global ownership for decades to come. Before you learn how to create, buy, sell, trade, collect, use, or even build businesses with NFTs, you must first understand why they exist—because the true value of NFTs is not in the pictures people share, but in the powerful shift toward digital property rights that they represent.

For the first time in history, a digital item can be **one-of-a-kind**. This is a dramatic departure from traditional digital files, which could be duplicated endlessly with no way to know which one was the original. NFTs solved a problem that the internet never could: the ability to confirm authenticity and ownership without relying on a central authority. A digital painting no longer needs a gallery to verify it. A virtual item in a game no longer disappears when a company shuts down. A diploma, ticket, membership card, collectible, or contract no longer needs a middleman to confirm whether it is real. Every NFT carries its own proof, baked directly into the blockchain, making it tamper-proof and trustless. This is why major industries—from entertainment to real estate to luxury goods—are quietly preparing for a world where NFTs serve as the universal language of ownership and digital identity.

But the rise of NFTs is not just technological; it is deeply cultural. Creativity has always needed a marketplace, but the internet struggled to give creators fair compensation. Artists watched their work circulate freely online with little control and no royalties. Musicians earned fractions of a penny for streams. Game creators built entire worlds only to watch platforms take the majority of the profit. NFTs flipped this model by allowing creators to embed royalties into their work, automate payments, and reach global audiences without relying on publishers, galleries, or record labels. For creators—artists, designers, musicians, developers, filmmakers, authors, and innovators—NFTs represent a kind of financial liberation. For collectors, NFTs represent access, status, utility, and investment. For businesses, they represent a new frontier of customer engagement, loyalty, and brand experience. This book will guide you through all of these layers so you can navigate the world of NFTs like an insider rather than a spectator.

NFTs also play a major role in the Metaverse, which you explored in Book 1, and in the broader Web3 ecosystem explained in Book 2. Inside virtual worlds, NFTs serve as the backbone of **ownership-based economies**. Avatars, clothing, vehicles, digital land, buildings, tools, accessories, special abilities, business licenses, and even entire revenue streams can all be tokenized as NFTs. Someone can build a store in the Metaverse and sell NFT items. A company can host a virtual event and issue NFT tickets. A musician can perform a concert and drop limited-edition NFT merchandise. A teacher can sell NFT-based course passes. A business can offer NFT membership tiers that unlock exclusive content and real-world benefits. These are not theories—they are happening now, and the most successful digital entrepreneurs of the next decade will be those who understand how NFTs shape the new economy.

Of course, the explosive growth of NFTs also created confusion, misinformation, and skepticism. Many people still believe NFTs are "just JPEGs." Others think the market is only speculation or that NFTs became irrelevant when the initial hype faded. But throughout history—whether with the internet, smartphones, or social media—early waves of experimentation often look chaotic before the true use cases emerge. The NFT market is now entering its maturity phase, where utility, identity, ownership, governance, gaming, and real-world integration matter far more than viral images. This book is written for this new era—one where NFTs are evolving into digital property rights for billions of people, and where understanding them gives you a tremendous advantage in the economy of Web3.

In the chapters ahead, you will learn exactly how NFTs work, from blockchain fundamentals to metadata, smart contracts, marketplaces, minting, wallets, gas fees, and utility-driven applications. You will discover how to evaluate NFTs like a professional, spotting red flags, understanding rarity, and analyzing long-term value. You will explore how to create your own NFTs—even if you have no technical skills—using both simple tools and advanced methods. You will also learn how NFTs are used in gaming, entertainment, real estate, branding, membership programs, fashion, sports, and decentralized communities. Just as importantly, you will learn about security, wallets, scams, copyrights, and legal considerations so you can navigate the space safely. Whether your goal is to create art, build a community, start a business, or become an investor, this book will give you every tool you need to participate with confidence.

This introduction is also an invitation. By choosing to learn about NFTs now, you are positioning yourself ahead of a global transformation. Web3 is shifting the internet from "platform-owned" to **user-owned**, and NFTs are a cornerstone of that shift. Ten years from now, most people will interact with NFTs without even realizing it—just like people use the internet today without understanding TCP/IP. Identity documents, home deeds, streaming passes, loyalty memberships, software licenses, resumes, certifications, and even personal medical records may all be NFT-based. Businesses that ignore NFTs will lose customers. Creators who understand NFTs will build empires. And individuals who take the time to master this technology now will enjoy opportunities that simply won't exist for late adopters. This book empowers you to be among the pioneers—not just observers—in the new digital economy.

As you begin this journey into the world of NFTs, remember that this space rewards curiosity, experimentation, and creativity. You do not need to be an artist, a coder, or a collector to succeed. You simply need to understand how NFTs work, why they matter, and how to use them strategically. By the end of this book, you'll not only understand NFTs—you'll know how to profit from them, create with them, invest in them, and participate in one of the most important technological shifts of your lifetime. Welcome to Book 3 of the *Metaverse Masterclass* series. Welcome to the world of digital ownership. And welcome to the next evolution of the internet.

Chapter 1

The Foundation Of NFTs

To understand NFTs at a high level, you must begin with the concept of uniqueness in the digital world. Traditionally, anything digital—images, videos, music files, documents, designs, game assets—could be copied endlessly without losing quality. This infinite replication made digital media useful but also made ownership impossible to verify. The internet lacked a way to say, "This specific digital item belongs to this specific person." NFTs, or non-fungible tokens, introduced the solution by creating a blockchain-based identity for a digital asset that cannot be duplicated, forged, or separated from its transaction history. At their core, NFTs are unique digital certificates that represent ownership of something, whether digital or physical. This breakthrough created a new class of digital property rights that works anywhere in the world, without relying on centralized companies.

To understand how NFTs work, you must understand why the blockchain is essential. A blockchain is a decentralized database controlled by no single entity. It records transactions in a permanent, transparent, and publicly verifiable way. When an NFT is minted—meaning created—it is assigned a token ID and a smart contract address. These two elements are permanently stored on the blockchain, making the NFT identifiable forever. Every future sale or transfer updates the blockchain, creating a chronological record of ownership. This is why NFTs cannot be faked or duplicated; any copy that isn't tied to the original smart contract simply has no value. The blockchain itself provides the authenticity, provenance, and trust that traditional digital files lacked.

But NFTs are not just digital images or pieces of art; they are tokenized assets. An NFT can represent almost anything: artwork, music, videos, domain names, virtual real estate, in-game items, digital clothing, event tickets, loyalty passes, identity documents, certifications, or even fractional ownership in real-world property. This flexibility is what makes NFTs groundbreaking. When people first heard of NFTs, they focused on profile pictures and generative art because they were the first mainstream use case. But beneath the surface, NFTs were always intended to unlock new business models: real-world asset tokenization, decentralized identity systems, creator royalties, programmable memberships, Web3 gaming economies, and new ways for communities and brands to interact with their audiences. NFTs are not a trend—they are an infrastructure layer for the next version of the internet.

To participate in the NFT ecosystem, you must understand smart contracts. A smart contract is a piece of code stored on the blockchain that automatically executes rules without needing human involvement. It defines what the NFT can do, how it can be transferred, whether it includes royalties for the creator, whether it unlocks access to exclusive content, and how it behaves in different marketplaces. Smart contracts are why NFTs are programmable assets rather than static files. They can evolve, grant permissions, reveal new features, or interact with other applications. For example, a smart contract may allow an NFT to grant membership to a club, unlock a digital course, upgrade inside a game, or gain additional traits as a player progresses. This programmability makes NFTs far more dynamic than traditional collectibles.

Next, you must understand wallets. A crypto wallet is your digital identity in Web3 and the place where your NFTs are stored. Wallets like MetaMask, Phantom, or Ledger act as your keys to interact with blockchains. You do not store the NFT inside the wallet in the same way you store photos on your phone. Instead, your wallet stores the cryptographic keys that prove you own the NFT recorded on the blockchain. Losing your wallet login or seed phrase is equivalent to losing the keys to a bank vault filled with valuables—there is no customer support to recover it. This is why wallet security is one of the most important concepts in the world of NFTs. Now you must understand minting. Minting is the process of transforming a digital file into an NFT by recording it on the blockchain. When you mint an NFT, the blockchain assigns it a unique identity, making it traceable and verifiable. Minting can be done using no-code platforms like OpenSea, Rarible, or Magic Eden, or by creating custom smart contracts with the help of developers or tools like Manifold. Minting typically requires gas fees, which are payments made to blockchain validators for processing and storing the transaction. Some blockchains offer low-cost minting, while others—like Ethereum—can require higher fees depending on network activity. Minting is the gateway through which artists, creators, businesses, and brands launch their NFT collections.

Finally, you must understand utility. The NFT space is moving far beyond collectibles. The most successful NFTs today—and in the future—will be those that offer utility, meaning they provide real-world or digital benefits beyond ownership. Utility can take many forms: access, membership, discounts, courses, streaming rights, physical products, event tickets, game perks, virtual land ownership, community participation, governance votes, and much more. In this book, you will learn how to analyze whether an NFT has strong utility, how to predict long-term value, and how to avoid NFTs that have no substance. The more useful an NFT is, the more valuable it becomes in the long run. Taken together, these concepts—uniqueness, blockchain verification, smart contracts, wallets, minting, and utility—give you the complete foundation you need to navigate NFTs with confidence. Whether you want to create your own collection, invest in undervalued assets, build a Web3 business, or enter the world of digital ownership on a professional level, this chapter forms the core understanding required to succeed. NFTs are not complicated once you see the logic behind them. They are simply digital assets powered by blockchain technology, governed by smart contracts, and enhanced by utility that can be expanded infinitely. As the rest of this book unfolds, you will learn how to use this technology to your advantage in the new Web3 economy.

"The Artist Who Could Not Be Copied"

Lena Morales never imagined her life would change because of a single digital file. She was a quiet illustrator who lived in a small apartment with more plants than furniture. Her art had always been the one place where she felt completely free—painting galaxies, floating cities, dream creatures, and worlds she wished she could escape to. She shared her work online, posting images that were vibrant and emotional, the kind of pieces people said should belong in galleries. But every time one of her illustrations went viral, it was copied thousands of times without her permission. Brands used it.

Influencers reposted it. Companies printed it on shirts. Her artwork spread everywhere, and yet Lena earned nothing from it. She felt invisible, like the world wanted her creations but didn't care about the creator.

One night, frustrated after discovering her art printed on a large website's merchandise without credit, she stumbled upon an online group discussing something called "NFTs." The comments were filled with arguments—some people calling them scams, others saying they were the future. Lena didn't understand any of it. But one line from a user caught her eye: "NFTs let artists finally own their digital work." Those words echoed in her mind all night. For the first time, something suggested that artists could protect their creations online. The next morning, curiosity pushed her into a rabbit hole. She learned that an NFT wasn't the artwork itself—it was the proof of ownership. A digital certificate saying, "This piece belongs to you." It didn't prevent people from saving copies, but it made those copies worthless. The original could always be verified.

Lena spent days learning about wallets, blockchains, and minting. She struggled at first—nothing made sense. Words like "gas fee," "smart contract," and "metadata" felt like an alien language. But slowly, piece by piece, she learned to navigate the space. She created a digital wallet and wrote her seed phrase on paper, hiding it inside a sketchbook. She uploaded one of her favorite illustrations—a glowing tree with cosmic veins—and pressed the mint button. In that moment, something shifted. The artwork she had created years earlier now had a digital identity that no one could steal. For the first time in her life, Lena felt like she owned her own work.

She didn't expect anyone to buy it. She wasn't famous. She wasn't a celebrity artist. She was just a woman with a laptop and a dream. But two days later, a notification popped up on her phone: "Your NFT has sold." Her heart stopped. Someone had purchased her artwork—not a print, not a license, but the original digital ownership—directly from her. She stared at her screen, tears forming as the reality hit her. For years, people had taken her art without permission. Now, someone valued her enough to pay for her creation in a way the internet had never allowed before.

As weeks passed, more of her NFTs sold. Collectors sent her messages thanking her for bringing beauty into the world. Other artists reached out, asking how she did it. For the first time, her art wasn't something the world took from her; it was something she controlled. She learned about royalties embedded in smart contracts. Every time one of her NFTs resold, she received money automatically—without lifting a finger. Her income began to grow, not because she was producing endlessly, but because her creations lived independently on the blockchain. They had their own lives, their own journey, their own collectors.

But the most powerful moment came when she joined a virtual gallery event in the Metaverse. People from around the world gathered as avatars, walking through a digital space filled with glowing art on large floating display screens. When Lena stepped into the virtual gallery, she saw her own work displayed among others. She watched as avatars stopped in front of her piece, discussing colors, symbolism, and emotion. She heard strangers admire it, analyze it, fall in love with it. For the first time in her life, she truly felt seen. Her work wasn't lost in the chaos of the internet—it was showcased, honored, and protected.

Lena understood then that NFTs were not just technology. They were empowerment. They were a way for creators to exist in a world that had ignored them. They were a way to give digital things a soul, a story, and a provenance that couldn't be erased. As she looked around the gallery, she realized every NFT had a journey—each one minted by someone with a dream. Owners stood beside her artwork not as exploiters but as supporters. Collectors. Patrons. People who believed in her vision enough to invest in it.

That night, as she closed her laptop, Lena made a promise to herself. She would not let her creativity be stolen again. She would mint more NFTs, build a community, and teach other artists how to protect and profit from their work. She finally understood what NFTs truly represented: not speculation, not hype, but **freedom**. A future where artists could own their creations, control their distribution, and receive fair compensation. A future where digital ownership mattered as much as physical ownership. A future where creators like her could not be erased, copied, or silenced.

NFTs gave her something that had been missing for years—dignity. And for Lena Morales, that was worth more than any sale.

Chapter 2

How Blockchains Power NFTs

To fully understand NFTs—and to use them confidently—you must first understand the engine that powers them: the blockchain. Without blockchain technology, NFTs could not be unique, secure, traceable, or digitally owned. At its core, a blockchain is a distributed ledger, meaning copies of its data are stored on thousands of computers around the world rather than one centralized server. This decentralization makes the blockchain resistant to hacking, fraud, or manipulation. When an NFT transaction is recorded on the blockchain, it cannot be altered or deleted. That transaction becomes part of a chronological chain of data that forms a permanent and transparent history of ownership. This is the foundation that gives NFTs their value—trust without needing a middleman.

Each blockchain operates based on consensus mechanisms, which are systems that allow all participants to agree on the validity of data. The two most common mechanisms are Proof of Work (PoW) and Proof of Stake (PoS). Ethereum originally used PoW, but later migrated to PoS to improve energy efficiency and scale. Bitcoin still uses PoW. Most modern NFT-focused blockchains—such as Solana, Polygon, Avalanche, and Tezos—use PoS because it allows faster transactions and lower fees. Understanding the difference matters because the blockchain you choose to mint on determines transaction costs, speed, security, and environmental impact. For example, minting on Ethereum may cost more in gas fees but grants wider exposure and marketplace compatibility, while minting on a chain like Polygon or Solana offers lower fees and faster processing with growing market adoption.

Each blockchain has its own programming language and smart contract standards. Ethereum uses the ERC-721 and ERC-1155 standards to create NFTs. ERC-721 represents single, unique items, while ERC-1155 can mint multiple items under one contract, making it ideal for gaming assets or collections with multiple copies. Solana uses SPL tokens; Polygon uses Ethereum-compatible standards; Tezos uses FA2. When you mint an NFT, you are creating a token that follows the rules of one of these standards, and those rules define how the NFT behaves. This structure ensures interoperability—meaning your NFT can function across marketplaces, wallets, and platforms built on that blockchain.

The metadata of an NFT is another essential concept. Metadata is the information that describes the NFT—its name, traits, attributes, description, image link, and any additional properties like levels, stats, or utility. Metadata can be stored on centralized servers, decentralized storage solutions like IPFS, or permanently on-chain. Storing metadata on centralized servers poses risk because the NFT's "image" or traits could disappear if that server shuts down. IPFS (InterPlanetary File System) solves this by distributing the data across many nodes, ensuring durability. On-chain metadata means everything—image included—is encoded directly into the blockchain, but this is rare due to storage limitations. Understanding metadata is critical because it determines the long-term stability and integrity of your NFT.

Another essential part of blockchains and NFTs is the relationship between wallets and public/private keys. Your wallet interacts with the blockchain using a pair of cryptographic keys: a public key, which acts like your receiving address, and a private key, which acts like your password. Whoever holds the private key effectively owns the assets inside the wallet. This is why "not your keys, not your crypto" is an important phrase in Web3. Wallets like MetaMask, Phantom, Trust Wallet, and Ledger don't store NFTs themselves—they store the private keys that allow you to access NFTs recorded on the blockchain. Ledger and other hardware wallets add protection by storing private keys offline, making them immune to online hacking attempts. Understanding keys and wallets is foundational for safely navigating the NFT space. Gas fees are another core component. Gas fees are payments made to blockchain validators for processing transactions. These fees depend on the network's activity and the computational power required. On Ethereum, gas fees can fluctuate from a few dollars to hundreds depending on demand. On chains like Solana or Polygon, gas fees typically cost a fraction of a cent. Gas fees exist to prevent network spam and ensure that validators are compensated for their work. When you mint, buy, sell, or transfer an NFT, you will usually pay a gas fee. Understanding gas helps you time your transactions and avoid unnecessary costs.

Lastly, you must understand blockchain explorers—tools like Etherscan, Solscan, and Polygonscan. These explorers allow you to verify any NFT, wallet address, transaction, or smart contract. If someone claims an NFT is rare, you can check the metadata. If someone claims they sent a payment, you can verify the transaction. If a collection claims a certain supply, you can confirm it directly on the blockchain. Explorers are the ultimate transparency tool of Web3 and empower you to verify every piece of information directly at the source.

When you combine all these components—blockchains, consensus mechanisms, smart contract standards, metadata, wallets, gas fees, and explorers—you get a complete picture of how NFTs function. This chapter provides the technological grounding that will allow you to navigate the NFT ecosystem with sophistication and confidence. Blockchains are the foundation of everything in Web3, and understanding their mechanics gives you the power to evaluate NFT collections, launch your own projects, invest wisely, and participate securely in the new digital economy.

"The Blockchain Map"

Kai Nakamura was the kind of person who believed in logic above all else. He was a computer science student, a quiet observer, a lover of puzzles, and someone who found comfort in systems that made sense. But Web3 had always confused him. The blockchain seemed like a chaotic concept—something people hyped without understanding. NFTs especially annoyed him. How could people spend money on JPEGs? How could something digital be worth anything? One evening, after overhearing classmates debate the future of cryptocurrencies, he decided he needed to see the truth for himself. Not because he wanted to join them, but because he hated not understanding something that everyone else seemed obsessed with.

He began by opening a blockchain explorer—Etherscan. The interface looked intimidating: wallet addresses, transaction IDs, block numbers, token trackers, gas fees. He felt lost. But something in him refused to walk away. He clicked on a random transaction and watched the data unfold. There it was: sender, receiver, timestamp, value, block confirmation, smart contract interaction. Every detail was public. Nothing was hidden. Every transfer anyone ever made was permanently visible, like footprints in wet cement. The more he explored, the more he realized this wasn't chaos—it was structure. It was order. It was a map. A global map of every digital action, linked together forever.

Over the next week, he studied how blockchains worked, spending long nights reading about decentralization, consensus mechanisms, and smart contracts. He learned that the blockchain wasn't controlled by any single company. Instead, it was run by thousands of independent computers, all verifying and agreeing on the same information. He had never seen anything like it. It was the opposite of traditional databases, which lived in private servers controlled by corporations. Here, transparency was the default. Nothing could be faked. Nothing could be deleted. This was truth encoded into mathematics.

One night, while reading about NFT standards like ERC-721, something clicked. NFTs were not the image. They were certificates. They were proof, backed by the blockchain, that a digital item was unique and owned by someone. If an image was copied a thousand times, it didn't matter—only one version had the verified stamp of authenticity. That stamp lived on the blockchain permanently, and anyone could check it. For the first time, digital ownership made sense to Kai. His curiosity pushed him further. He downloaded MetaMask and generated his first wallet. The random string of words—his seed phrase—felt strange in his hands, as if he held a key to an invisible vault. He wrote it down carefully. He explored gas fees, learning how they surged during peak hours and dropped when the network was calm. He minted a test NFT on a low-fee blockchain just to see how it worked. When the transaction confirmed, he opened the explorer again. There it was: his wallet, the contract address, the token ID, the metadata. A permanent record that he had created something on the blockchain.

But the moment everything changed was when he discovered decentralized storage. He uploaded a small artwork to IPFS and realized the file wasn't stored on one server—it was stored across a network. No single company could delete it. No one could censor it. The blockchain stored its location; IPFS stored its data. It was a partnership between permanence and distribution. Kai sat back, staring at the screen, overwhelmed by the elegance of it all. The blockchain wasn't just a ledger. It was a new kind of digital infrastructure, one where trust wasn't required because verification was built in.

One evening, he joined a virtual meetup for developers in a Metaverse environment. People from different countries appeared as avatars, discussing how they built NFT games, membership passes, generative art, identity tools, and more. Kai listened silently, absorbing everything. He realized that each of these creators was using the blockchain as a canvas. Smart contracts were their brushes. Tokens were their colors. Transparency was their foundation. For the first time, Kai understood that NFTs were not about the pictures—they were about what the pictures represented.

As he left the virtual space, he checked the NFT he had minted earlier. It wasn't beautiful. It wasn't valuable. It wasn't meant to be. But it was proof that he had learned something profound. The blockchain wasn't confusing anymore. It was a map. A living map of digital history, identity, and ownership—and he had drawn something on it. Kai closed his laptop with a newfound sense of clarity. He finally understood what the world was building, and he wanted to be part of it.

Chapter 3

How NFTs Are Created: The Minting Process

To participate in the world of NFTs—whether as a creator, investor, or builder—you must understand the minting process. Minting is the moment a digital asset becomes an NFT. It is the transformation from a normal file into a blockchain-verified, one-of-a-kind token with its own identity, provenance, and history. Before minting, a digital image, audio file, video, or item has no uniqueness. It's simply a file that can be copied. After minting, it becomes a tracked digital asset with ownership recorded on the blockchain, forever distinguishable from counterfeits. This process is what gives NFTs their power. To master NFTs, you must master minting.

The first step in minting an NFT is choosing the blockchain. This decision impacts everything—from transaction fees to community size to marketplace compatibility. Ethereum remains the most widely recognized blockchain for NFTs, known for its established marketplace ecosystem, collector base, and premium valuation. However, gas fees on Ethereum can be high. Polygon offers Ethereum compatibility with significantly lower fees. Solana offers speed and low cost, making it a favorite for generative art and gaming. Tezos,

Avalanche, Immutable, and other chains each serve niche communities. The blockchain you choose affects where your NFT will live and which audiences you can reach. For beginners, Polygon or Solana offers a low-cost way to experiment; for premium collections, Ethereum remains the gold standard.

The second step is preparing your digital asset. NFT files can be images, GIFs, videos, audio clips, PDFs, 3D models, virtual items, or interactive media. The file itself is not stored on the blockchain due to size limitations. Instead, the NFT contains a pointer—a link—to where the file is stored, usually on decentralized storage like IPFS or Arweave. Before minting, creators must ensure the file is final, high-quality, and properly formatted. Once minted, any change to the file would require minting a new NFT.

The third step involves metadata creation. Metadata is the structured information that describes the NFT, stored either on-chain or via decentralized storage linked to the token. Metadata includes the NFT's name, description, attributes, rarity traits, levels, stats, category, and external links. For generative collections, metadata defines the uniqueness of each item—for example, the character's background color, clothing, accessories, rarity percentage, or special traits. Metadata is critical because collectors evaluate NFTs based on traits and rarity. Good metadata adds clarity, structure, and long-term value to an NFT.

The fourth step is choosing how to mint. There are three primary minting methods: (1) **Minting on a no-code platform** like OpenSea, Rarible, Magic Eden, or Objkt, which is the easiest option for beginners. These platforms allow creators to upload files, define metadata, pay a small gas fee, and instantly create an NFT. (2) **Lazy minting**, where the NFT is not written to the blockchain until someone buys it, allowing creators to avoid upfront gas fees. (3) **Custom smart contract minting**, which is ideal for large collections, advanced features, or branded projects. Smart contract platforms like Manifold, Thirdweb, or custom Solidity development allow full control over royalties, reveals, on-chain logic, and advanced features.

The fifth step is minting the NFT itself. Once the smart contract is ready and the file is uploaded, the creator sends a transaction to the blockchain. This transaction includes the mint function, which assigns the NFT a token ID and registers it under the creator's wallet address. Gas fees are paid at this moment. After confirmation, the NFT appears in the creator's wallet and in the blockchain explorer. It now exists permanently, with its own distinct address and provenance. The sixth step is setting royalties. Royalties are one of the defining advantages of NFTs for creators. A creator can embed a royalty percentage—typically 5% to 10%—so that every time the NFT is resold in the future, they receive earnings automatically. While some marketplaces have changed enforcement methods, royalties still represent a powerful ongoing income stream for many artists and brands. Setting royalties requires specifying the percentage in the smart contract or in the platform's royalty settings.

The seventh step is listing and selling the NFT. Minting does not automatically list your NFT for sale. You must choose a marketplace, set a price, choose between fixed pricing, auction, or declining-price mechanisms, and define visibility. Marketplaces vary by blockchain and audience: OpenSea for general collections, Magic Eden for Solana and Bitcoin Ordinals, Blur for experienced traders, Exchange Art for fine-art collectors, and Foundation for curated creator communities. Listing also requires a small gas fee depending on the blockchain.

The final part of the minting process involves understanding ownership transfer. When a buyer acquires your NFT, the blockchain records the transfer from your wallet to theirs. The NFT remains the same object, but its owner changes. Future transfers continue to update the blockchain, forming an immutable chain of custody. Ownership is not symbolic—it is verified cryptographically and publicly, giving NFTs a level of transparency unmatched in traditional markets.

By mastering the minting process, you unlock the ability to tokenize your creativity, build a digital brand, or launch large-scale NFT collections. Minting is the gateway to the entire NFT economy. Whether you are a creator minting your first artwork or an entrepreneur building a 10,000-item collection, understanding these steps ensures your NFTs are secure, functional, and optimized for long-term success. Minting is more than uploading a file—it is the act of bringing digital property to life.

"The First Mint"

The day Maya decided to mint her first NFT, she felt like she was standing at the edge of a cliff. She wasn't a famous artist or a tech expert. She was a 27-year-old graphic designer who spent her days freelancing and her nights experimenting with surreal digital illustrations. Her art had always been her escape—vivid dreamscapes, glowing mountains, and characters made of stardust. People liked her posts on social media, but nothing ever changed. No gallery recognition. No financial stability. No sense of growth. But when she heard about NFTs, something inside her sparked. Maybe, she thought, this was her chance to finally do something big with her work. For a week she immersed herself in learning. She watched tutorials. She joined Discord servers. She scrolled through OpenSea listings and wondered how ordinary people were making money selling digital art. The idea fascinated her. Digital art that you could actually own? A marketplace for creativity where middlemen didn't take all the value? It felt unreal. But the part that terrified her the most was minting. The idea of writing something onto the blockchain—a place she imagined as a glowing universe of code—felt overwhelming. She wasn't sure she was ready. She wasn't even sure she belonged in this new world.

One night, she opened her favorite artwork: a glowing figure made of shifting constellations, standing under a neon moon. She stared at it, feeling something she hadn't felt in years—pride. Maybe it was time. She created a wallet, carefully writing down her seed phrase on a piece of paper. Her hands trembled as she typed the words into the recovery field, confirming she understood the responsibility. She uploaded her file. She added the title: "Starborn." She wrote a description that felt honest: "A reminder that even in darkness, we are made of light." She felt her chest tighten as she moved through the steps. She wasn't just uploading a file. She was turning a piece of her heart into something the world could own.

She hesitated when the mint button appeared. Her finger hovered over the mouse. She heard her doubts whisper: *This is silly. This is risky. You'll waste money. No one will buy it.* But then she felt something else—courage. She clicked. A transaction window popped up. Gas fees were higher than she expected, but she pressed confirm anyway. The screen showed: *Pending.* Her entire body froze as the seconds dragged on. Then, finally: *Transaction Confirmed.* Her heart raced. It existed. It was real. Her artwork was now on the blockchain as an NFT, with its own identity and token number. She checked her wallet, and there it was—"Starborn #1." For the first time in her life, her art didn't feel disposable.

Every few minutes she refreshed her listing, wondering if anyone would even see it. Hours passed. Nothing. She tried to distract herself, but her mind kept circling back. When she finally fell asleep, her laptop was still open beside her. The next morning she woke to a notification that nearly made her scream. "Your NFT has sold." She couldn't process it at first. Someone—a stranger from another part of the world—had bought her art. Not downloaded it. Not screenshotted it. *Bought it.* Her eyes filled with tears. She clicked the buyer's profile. They had a small collection of indie creators—artists just like her. They sent her a message: "Your work is beautiful. Please keep creating."

Maya sat at her desk, unable to stop smiling. It wasn't just about the money. It was the validation. The connection. The knowledge that her art mattered enough for someone to want to own it. She realized minting wasn't about technology—it was about taking ownership of your creativity and giving it a place in the world. The blockchain wasn't cold or impersonal. It was a living record of human expression.

That night, she opened a new canvas. She didn't feel intimidated anymore. She felt powerful. Minting her first NFT wasn't the end—it was the beginning. A gateway to a digital future where her creativity had value, visibility, and permanence. She saw a long road ahead: collections, communities, collaborations, maybe even her own NFT brand. For the first time in years, she believed in her art again. And all it took was one brave click on the mint button.

Chapter 4

How NFT Ownership Works

To truly master NFTs, you must understand how ownership works on a blockchain level. NFT ownership is fundamentally different from traditional digital ownership. When you buy a movie on a streaming platform, you do not truly own it—you purchase a license that can be revoked, altered, or restricted at any time. When you buy a video game skin inside a closed system, you cannot transfer it, resell it, or prove authenticity outside that platform. With NFTs, ownership is not granted by a company. It is enforced by cryptography. It exists independently of any platform, app, marketplace, or company that displays or hosts the NFT. This independence is what gives NFTs their power. Ownership belongs to the wallet that controls the private key—and only that wallet.

Every NFT exists as a token on a blockchain. That token is linked to a smart contract that defines the collection and manages all transfers. When you purchase an NFT, the blockchain records your wallet address as the owner. This "digital deed" cannot be forged, modified, or deleted. Unlike traditional digital goods, NFT ownership is permissionless, global, portable, and transparent. Anyone can verify your ownership using a blockchain explorer by checking the token

ID and wallet address. Ownership does not depend on the marketplace where you bought it. If OpenSea disappears, your NFT does not. If a platform shuts down, your NFT remains on the blockchain. This is the first step in understanding the long-term value of Web3: your assets do not belong to a company—they belong to you.

Understanding this ownership model also means recognizing what an NFT does *not* give you by default. Owning an NFT does not automatically grant you copyright, commercial rights, or intellectual property rights unless the collection explicitly states so. Some collections, like Bored Ape Yacht Club, grant full commercial rights to the owner. Others grant limited use. Some grant no rights at all beyond display. Reading the project's licensing terms is critical, as the rights you receive vary widely. Ownership of the token is not the same as ownership of the underlying artwork or asset unless the smart contract or license states otherwise. This distinction is one of the most misunderstood parts of NFTs and must be mastered to avoid legal or ethical mistakes.

Another important component of NFT ownership is utility-based access. Many NFTs function like membership keys, unlocking gated Discord channels, exclusive websites, virtual worlds, events, or premium content. Your wallet acts as your access pass. When a website checks your NFT ownership, it simply verifies the blockchain to confirm the wallet connected to the site contains the specific token required. This verification process is what enables decentralized authentication, often called “token-gated access.” As Web3 evolves, more businesses, courses, communities, creators, and brands will use NFTs as access credentials. Ownership becomes a key to experiences, perks, and digital identities.

Ownership also extends to royalty mechanisms. When a creator mints an NFT collection, they can embed royalties that automatically trigger upon resale. These royalties are not paid manually—they are coded into the smart contract. Whenever the NFT is transferred through a compliant marketplace, the blockchain executes the royalty payment. Although some marketplaces have altered default royalty enforcement, creators still widely benefit from this system, particularly in ecosystems that respect on-chain royalties. This creates a continuous revenue stream for artists and project founders, rewarding long-term creation rather than one-time sales.

Another dimension of NFT ownership is provenance—the historical chain of ownership. Provenance matters because the blockchain records every transfer from the moment of minting. Collectors place high value on NFTs once owned by prominent individuals, brands, or founders. Provenance acts as a transparent, tamper-proof biography of the NFT. This feature is especially important for art, luxury assets, and items with historical significance. Unlike physical art, where provenance can be forged, disputed, or lost, NFT provenance is permanent and indisputable.

Security is another critical part of understanding ownership. Because ownership depends on controlling a private key, losing that key—or exposing it—means losing your NFT forever. There is no "forgot password" option. There is no customer service line for recovery. Scams, phishing attacks, fake minting links, and malicious smart contracts are prevalent in Web3. This is not because NFTs are unsafe, but because ownership in this world is true ownership—meaning you are entirely responsible for safeguarding your assets. Hardware wallets drastically improve safety by keeping private keys offline. Learning to verify smart contracts, double-check URLs, and use cold storage solutions is essential for every serious NFT collector or creator.

Finally, NFT ownership gives you the ability to transfer, gift, fractionalize, or leverage your asset in DeFi. Smart contracts allow you to divide ownership into multiple parts, use NFTs as collateral for loans, stake them in governance systems, or integrate them into digital ecosystems. Ownership is not passive—it can be dynamic, interactive, and financial. The future of NFTs will include identity passports, tokenized real estate deeds, academic credentials, medical records, and business contracts. Each of these will rely on blockchain-based ownership for security and accessibility.

Understanding NFT ownership at this deeper level allows you to navigate the ecosystem like a professional. It empowers you to identify valuable projects, avoid scams, understand long-term implications, and leverage your NFTs in ways most newcomers never consider. Ownership is the foundation of Web3, and mastering it is essential to your success in the digital economy.

"The Token That Chose Its Owner"

Ethan Ruiz never cared much for digital collectibles. He was a practical person—someone who believed only in what he could hold. His apartment was neatly arranged with books, guitars, and travel souvenirs. Everything he owned had a story. He liked things with weight, texture, and meaning. So when his friend Lucas kept talking about NFTs, Ethan brushed it off. "Why would I buy something I can't touch?" he would say. But the question that haunted him later wasn't why he should buy one—it was why he couldn't stop thinking about them.

One evening, Lucas invited him to a gallery event in a virtual world. Ethan agreed reluctantly, expecting something unimpressive. Instead, he stepped into a digital space filled with glowing sculptures, shifting murals, and animated canvases that moved like they were alive. People walked around as avatars, discussing the artists, bidding on pieces, admiring the creativity. And then Ethan saw it—the piece that made his heart pause. A pulsating geometric cube floating midair, changing colors with every rotation, each color representing a memory encoded into the artwork. The piece felt...alive. As if it was watching him. It was called "Inheritance."

He moved closer to read its description. The artist wrote that the cube contained fragments of stories passed down through generations, preserved in color, geometry, and motion. Something about it resonated with Ethan. He had lost his grandmother the year before—the person who had given him his love for music, stories, and culture. He felt an emotional pull unlike anything he'd felt toward digital art before. Lucas nudged him. "You should buy it," he whispered. Ethan hesitated. Buying something digital still felt strange. But deep down, he sensed this moment was different.

After hours of thinking, he finally made his decision. He connected his wallet, confirmed the transaction, and watched as the blockchain processed the transfer. Within seconds, the glowing artwork belonged to him. He stared at his screen, unable to believe how real it felt. Ownership wasn't about physical weight—it was about connection. The art felt like an heirloom, something meant for him. He closed the gallery and sat quietly, overwhelmed by the feeling that something had chosen him.

Over the next few weeks, he learned more about NFT ownership. He discovered that he could verify his ownership on the blockchain by checking the token's unique ID. He learned how the smart contract ensured his purchase was permanent and immutable. He realized that no company or gallery could remove it, censor it, or claim it. It wasn't stored on a server that might disappear—it lived on a decentralized network, protected by thousands of nodes around the world. The artwork belonged to him more securely than anything he owned physically.

One day the artist reached out with a message: "Thank you for choosing 'Inheritance.' That piece was inspired by the stories my grandmother used to tell me. I'm glad it's with someone who understands it." Ethan felt a lump in his throat. He replied with gratitude, telling her how the piece connected with his own memories. They began talking regularly, bonding over shared experiences and creative perspectives. For the first time, Ethan understood what digital ownership really meant. It wasn't about files or pixels. It was about connection, story, and emotion preserved through technology.

Months later, he used "Inheritance" to access a private digital event hosted by the artist. The NFT acted as his ticket—his key. Without owning it, he wouldn't have been allowed to enter. Inside the virtual space, he met musicians, creators, collectors, and thinkers from around the world. He realized then that NFT ownership wasn't passive—it opened doors. It granted access. It created community. It forged relationships he never expected.

One evening, after attending a live virtual concert only accessible to holders of certain NFTs, he stood in his apartment staring at his physical possessions. Suddenly he noticed something. The guitar, the books, the souvenirs—they all held memories. But so did the glowing cube displayed on his monitor. It wasn't any less real just because he couldn't touch it. It meant something. And meaning, he realized, was the true essence of ownership.

Years from now, when people asked him why he believed in NFTs, he always told the same story: that ownership is not about weight—it's about connection. That a digital token had taught him something no physical object ever could. And that sometimes, the things meant for us find us in places we least expect. "Inheritance" wasn't just an NFT. It was the first digital heirloom he ever owned.

Chapter 5

NFT Utilities & Use Cases

NFTs began as digital collectibles, but their true power lies in the utility they provide. Utility is the set of benefits, functions, or uses that owning an NFT grants you. It can be digital, physical, financial, experiential, social, or technological. Utility is what separates NFTs with long-term value from NFTs driven purely by speculation. Understanding utility is essential for identifying high-potential projects, building your own NFT collections, or using NFTs in your business. While art-based NFTs remain influential, the larger story is how NFTs are transforming industries such as gaming, finance, entertainment, education, events, ticketing, real estate, branding, and online communities. To truly grasp the future of Web3, you must understand NFT utility deeply—not just what exists today, but what is rapidly being built.

The most common form of utility is **access utility**, where NFTs function as membership passes. Token-gated access allows NFT holders to enter exclusive online communities, private Discord groups, premium content portals, mastermind groups, mctaverse worlds, or real-life events. A wallet serves as the authentication method. If the wallet contains the NFT, access is granted automatically. This model replaces traditional username/password systems with blockchain verification. Projects like proof-of-membership clubs, VIP tiers, artist fan communities, online learning academies, and conference passes all use NFTs to verify identity and membership. This system is far more secure and flexible than traditional password-based access.

Another form of utility is **ownership utility**, where NFTs represent rights, licenses, certifications, or property. An NFT can represent ownership of digital assets like virtual land, in-game items, or domain names. But NFTs can also represent physical assets such as houses, cars, luxury items, certificates, diplomas, warranties, business shares, or fractionalized real estate. Because the blockchain is immutable, the ownership record is accurate, transparent, and easily transferable. This eliminates the need for paper deeds, notaries, or intermediaries. Real estate tokenization is already taking shape, and major industries are preparing to adopt NFTs for future ownership systems.

One of the most important forms of NFT utility is **financial utility**, where NFTs combine with DeFi (decentralized finance). In this model, NFTs can be staked for rewards, used as collateral for loans, traded for yield, or integrated into liquidity pools. A rare NFT can be locked in a DeFi protocol as collateral to borrow tokens without selling the asset. This turns

NFTs into productive financial instruments. Dynamic NFTs can evolve based on user activity, providing upgraded financial benefits for long-term holders. Bonding curves and automated market makers (AMMs) also allow NFTs to be bought and sold through algorithmic pricing models. These mechanisms create entire financial ecosystems around NFTs.

In the world of gaming, NFTs provide **functional utility**, meaning they serve as game items, characters, skins, weapons, properties, vehicles, or resources that players can use inside virtual environments. Unlike traditional games, where all items are controlled by a central company, NFT-based games allow players to truly own their items. Players can buy, sell, or trade items freely, use them across multiple games, or upgrade them over time. Play-to-earn models reward users for gameplay with tokens or NFTs, creating new digital economies. This ownership-based gaming economy breaks the old "walled garden" model and gives players real earning potential.

NFTs also offer **identity utility**, allowing holders to build digital identities. Profile picture (PFP) NFTs like CryptoPunks and Bored Ape Yacht Club are not just avatars—they are status symbols, brand assets, and identity artifacts. People use them to build their online personas, similar to how people choose fashion, brands, or personal styles in the real world. As more social platforms integrate wallet authentication, NFTs will become the foundation of digital identity across Web3. Ownership becomes a form of digital self-expression and branding.

Another important category is **commercial rights utility**, where owning an NFT grants you the legal right to use the artwork or asset commercially. Some collections allow holders to create merchandise, stories, products, or brands around their NFTs. Others grant shared IP rights, enabling community-driven brands and decentralized creative projects. This utility model transforms NFTs into business-building tools, empowering creators and entrepreneurs to launch brands without negotiating traditional licensing agreements.

NFTs also provide **event utility**, where they function as digital tickets for concerts, conferences, sports events, and virtual meetups. Unlike traditional tickets, NFT tickets cannot be counterfeited, can track attendance, can provide collectible value, and can unlock post-event perks or digital memorabilia. Event organizers can also earn royalties on resale. This system solves long-standing issues like fraud, scalping, and unverifiable attendance.

The next generation of NFT utility lies in **dynamic and programmable NFTs**, where the NFT evolves over time based on user activity, performance, achievements, or external data. A dynamic NFT might change attributes when a task is completed, when market prices shift, or when real-world events occur. These NFTs create engaging, interactive experiences across loyalty programs, fitness apps, educational platforms, and metaverse ecosystems.

Understanding these categories—access, ownership, financial, functional, identity, commercial rights, event, and dynamic utility—prepares you to see NFTs not as isolated digital tokens but as a technology that will underpin the digital economy. Utility is the key to lasting value, and projects that deliver meaningful utility are the ones that will thrive as the NFT space matures. As industries adopt NFTs, utility-based models will dominate, and the most successful participants will be those who understand how to identify, design, and leverage utility at every level.

"The Key That Opened Everything"

Jasmine Carter had always felt like she was standing outside the world she wanted to be part of. She was ambitious, creative, and full of ideas, but every room she entered seemed to require connections she didn't have. Every opportunity seemed locked behind invisible doors. That changed the day she received an unexpected message from an online acquaintance: "I'm sending you something. It's a gift. Don't sell it. Use it."

She opened her wallet and saw it—a glowing NFT shaped like a golden digital key. The design was elegant: circuit patterns wrapped around the edges, a shimmering gem in the center, and a title beneath it: **"Keystone Pass — Tier One."** She didn't understand what it meant, but she sensed it wasn't ordinary. When she clicked the details, she discovered it granted access to a private creator network—a place she had heard about but never dared to dream she could enter. Membership was normally thousands of dollars. But her NFT granted full access.

She connected her wallet to the site. Instantly, the interface transformed. Exclusive forums appeared. Livestream replays unlocked. Masterclass libraries opened. Event invites displayed with RSVP buttons. She felt like she had been given the keys to a hidden kingdom. She joined her first live session hesitantly, expecting to feel out of place. Instead, she was welcomed warmly. "You must be new," someone said, smiling. "Welcome to the Keystone Circle." She felt her chest tighten with emotion. For the first time, she belonged somewhere extraordinary.

As weeks passed, she learned that her NFT wasn't just a pass—it was a multi-layered tool. It unlocked virtual events, private webinars, mentorship circles, business templates, and even co-working sessions inside metaverse environments. One day she used it to attend a digital conference that would have cost hundreds of dollars without the NFT. Another day she used it to claim a free merch drop exclusively for Keystone members. She was astonished. Every time she checked the NFT's utilities, something new had been added.

But the moment she realized the full power of utility was when she joined a metaverse workshop hosted by a well-known entrepreneur she admired. The room was filled with creators, artists, developers, and innovators from around the world. Jasmine listened silently at first, amazed by how open people were. At the end of the session, the host made an announcement: "I'm offering a collaboration opportunity to Keystone Pass holders only. Submit your project ideas, and we'll select three to fund."

Her heart pounded. She had an idea—a platform that helped underrepresented young creators find mentorship. She submitted her proposal without expecting anything. Two days later, she received a message: "Your project has been selected. Congratulations. Let's build something great." Tears streamed down her face. This wasn't luck. This was access—real access—granted by a digital token she barely understood a month earlier.

As she developed her project, she learned even more about NFT utility. The Keystone Pass acted as an identity badge, proving her membership wherever she went. It granted voting rights in community decisions, allowing her to help steer the network's direction. It offered commercial rights for specific assets in the Keystone ecosystem, enabling her to use the logo in her project's branding. Her NFT even evolved dynamically—upgrading visually as she completed workshops, attended events, and contributed to the community.

She began to see NFTs not as pictures, but as programmable passports—keys that opened doors she never knew existed. Her confidence grew. She hosted her own workshop one day, teaching others how she used utility NFTs to accelerate her career. People listened. They asked questions. They thanked her afterward. She realized she was no longer standing outside the world she wanted to join. She was shaping it.

Months later, she received another message from the acquaintance who had gifted her the NFT. "I knew you'd do something great with it," he wrote. She replied with gratitude, telling him how that one token changed the course of her life. The key had not only opened doors—it had opened her potential. And as she stared at the glowing NFT in her wallet, she understood something profound: utility wasn't just a feature. It was a bridge. A bridge between who she was and who she could become.

Chapter 6

NFT Marketplaces & Buying Strategies

NFT marketplaces are the core environments where NFTs are discovered, bought, sold, traded, analyzed, and valued. Understanding how these marketplaces function is essential for navigating the Web3 economy, whether you want to invest, collect, evaluate opportunities, or list your own NFTs. Unlike traditional e-commerce sites, NFT marketplaces operate on blockchain transactions, smart contracts, and wallet-based authentication. They are transparent, decentralized, and global, and each marketplace specializes in different types of assets, artistic cultures, and community-driven ecosystems. Mastering how marketplace dynamics work allows you to avoid risks, identify undervalued assets, and make strategic decisions that build long-term digital wealth.

Marketplace categories vary widely. **Open marketplaces**, such as OpenSea, Blur, Magic Eden, and LooksRare, allow anyone to mint, list, or purchase NFTs. These platforms dominate trading volume and attract both beginners and professional traders. OpenSea remains the most widely used general marketplace for Ethereum and Polygon, while Magic Eden leads on Solana and also supports Bitcoin Ordinals. Blur attracts advanced traders with features like portfolio bidding, analytics dashboards, and reward incentives. These marketplaces focus on liquidity, fast execution, and broad accessibility. **Curated marketplaces**, such as Foundation, SuperRare, Nifty Gateway, and MakersPlace, focus on high-quality, limited-edition digital art. Creators must apply or be invited, making these platforms similar to exclusive digital galleries. These sites are ideal for artists who want serious collectors and long-term valuation.

There are also **specialized marketplaces**, which serve specific niches. For example, Exchange Art focuses on Solana fine art. Objkt dominates Tezos-based art and collectibles. Immutable Marketplace specializes in gaming NFTs. Domain-specific platforms like ENS Domains or Unstoppable Domains focus on blockchain domain names. There are marketplaces for generative art, photography, gaming items, digital fashion, music NFTs, and more. Learning the cultural differences between marketplaces is critical. For example, Ethereum art collectors behave differently from Solana collectors. Gaming NFT holders differ from PFP communities. Each ecosystem has its own culture, expectations, and evaluation standards.

Before buying an NFT, you must understand the **verification process**. Verified collections on marketplaces typically have a blue checkmark or equivalent badge, indicating the collection is authentic. However, verification is not perfect, and fraudulent collections still appear. Always cross-check a collection's official links—Twitter, Discord, website, and smart contract address. Verify the contract address using the project's official communications. Never buy from newly published or unofficial collections without due diligence. Scammers often copy trending NFT projects to trick newcomers.

Once the collection is verified, evaluate the **market data**, including floor price, total supply, holder distribution, listing ratio, volume, and price history. The floor price is the lowest price at which an NFT from the collection is listed. A rising floor suggests demand; a falling floor indicates declining interest. Holder distribution matters because concentrated ownership—where a few wallets hold large percentages—creates risk of mass sell-offs. Healthy collections have a wide distribution of holders. Listing ratio—the percentage of NFTs currently listed for sale—reveals seller pressure. Low listing ratios indicate strong conviction among holders. Daily and weekly trading volume shows whether a collection is active or stagnant. Avoid collections with sudden artificial spikes or wash-trading patterns.

The next step is analyzing **rarity and traits**. Most NFT collections include attributes that vary in rarity. Rarity affects price significantly. Use rarity tools such as Rarity Sniper, Trait Sniper, HowRare.is (for Solana), or marketplace-built rarity rankings. While rarity is important, it should not be the only factor influencing your decision. Emotional appeal, cultural resonance, artist reputation, utility, and long-term roadmaps are equally crucial. Some of the best-performing NFTs historically were not rare—they were desirable for identity, symbolism, or utility. Rarity provides an edge, but it is not the entire equation.

Once you understand the collection, evaluate the **team and roadmap**. Successful NFT projects are rarely anonymous endeavors. Study the founders' history, their transparency, past accomplishments, community engagement, and execution ability. Projects that promise everything but deliver nothing are red flags. Look for verifiable team identities, realistic roadmaps, consistent communication, and examples of delivered utility. Rug pulls—projects abandoned by their creators—often show early signs, such as vague goals, no real product direction, and disappearing social activity. Serious projects maintain consistent momentum, even during bear markets.

When buying an NFT, focus on **entry strategies**. One strategy is the "floor sweep," where you buy NFTs at the floor price of a promising collection. This helps you enter at the lowest cost with the least risk. Another strategy is "trait sniping," where you look for undervalued rare traits that are priced below their rarity rank. This requires patience and market knowledge. A third strategy is "event-driven buying," where you purchase ahead of major announcements, utility releases, upgrades, or new partnerships. Finally, some collectors focus on buying directly from mint when the project is new, though mints can be risky if hype outweighs fundamentals.

You must also learn **exit strategies**. NFT markets are volatile, and knowing when to sell is just as important as when to buy. Use tiered listing strategies—listing multiple NFTs at different prices to gradually take profit while maintaining exposure. Monitor marketplace activity using analytics tools like Nansen, NFTGo, icy.tools, SolanaFloor, or Blur analytics. Sell into strength, not panic. When a collection experiences a surge in volume or price, consider taking partial profits. If the project loses momentum permanently, exit quickly. NFTs require active management for serious investors.

Last, always rely on **safe purchasing practices**. Use marketplace links from official project announcements. Double-check contract addresses before buying. Never approve unlimited spending permissions on unknown contracts. Use hardware wallets for high-value NFTs. Turn off marketplace bidding permissions when not needed. Many hacks occur not through minting, but through approving malicious contracts. Understanding NFT marketplaces and buying strategies allows you to navigate the space like a professional. You learn not only how to buy, but *why* to buy, *when* to buy, and *when* to walk away. Markets reward intelligence, patience, and discipline—and mastering these principles empowers you to build a successful portfolio in the Web3 economy.

"The Bidding Room"

Noah Bennett had always been fascinated by rare things. Limited-edition sneakers. Vintage cameras. First-edition books. His apartment was a museum of items that held stories. But when he discovered NFTs, he felt something new—something deeper. Digital collectibles confused him at first, but his curiosity refused to fade. One night, scrolling through social media, he stumbled upon a post from a digital art collective announcing an upcoming auction. The artwork previewed was mesmerizing—a shifting portrait called "The Whispering Face," created by an artist named Liora Ashen. The piece depicted a face made of smoke and light, constantly transforming in subtle, beautiful movements. Noah felt drawn to it immediately.

He clicked the link, which led to a curated marketplace he had never used before. The site displayed the auction time, the current bid, the bidding mechanics, and the NFT's details. But what caught his attention most was the description: "This artwork evolves over time based on the owner's interactions." Noah raised an eyebrow. *Evolves?* How could artwork evolve? But the more he read, the more intrigued he became. This wasn't a static image. It was a living, dynamic NFT that changed based on the actions of the person who owned it. He felt something stir inside him—a familiar feeling he experienced when he saw art that spoke directly to him.

When the auction opened, he sat at his desk with his wallet connected, his heart racing. Bids appeared instantly. The numbers climbed. He hesitated at first, watching others compete. But then he imagined losing the piece and regretting it forever. He made his first bid. His hands shook. Another user outbid him within seconds. He bid again. The room felt electric even though he was alone in his apartment. Bid after bid appeared. Noah felt his pulse speeding up. He was no longer buying digital art—he was chasing a piece of himself.

As the timer approached zero, Noah placed his final bid, pushing his limit. The screen froze for a moment, and his breath caught. Then the confirmation appeared: **"You are the winner."** He closed his eyes and exhaled slowly, a mixture of disbelief and exhilaration washing over him. He opened the NFT page. His wallet address appeared as the owner. The artwork glowed faintly, almost like it recognized him. He watched it for minutes, unable to look away. The face in the portrait seemed to shift more subtly now, as if awakening. Over the next days, something strange happened. The artwork evolved. At first it was minor—the tones deepened, the details sharpened. Then new symbols appeared in the smoke. He messaged the artist out of curiosity, asking how it worked. Liora responded warmly, explaining that the NFT used dynamic metadata that updated based on wallet interactions—holding, transferring, or staking the NFT produced different visual evolutions. Noah felt awe. This was not art you displayed. It was art you lived with.

He soon discovered the marketplace had additional features—analytics, rarity scores, provenance histories. He studied the bidding logs, noticing how many people had tried to win the piece. The auction room had been filled with collectors who saw its value. But somehow, the portrait had ended up with him. That thought made him feel connected to something bigger. He wasn't just an owner—he was part of the artwork's story now.

One day, as he browsed other marketplaces out of curiosity, he realized how much he had learned unintentionally. He could identify real collections versus fake ones. He understood traits, floor prices, and listing behaviors. He could spot undervalued pieces. He could analyze team credibility. He wasn't just a collector anymore. He was becoming a strategist. And it all began because a piece of art had called to him.

Months later, the marketplace hosted a virtual exhibit featuring all of Liora's dynamic pieces. Noah attended, standing in the digital gallery with dozens of avatars. Suddenly, Liora's voice echoed through the room: "I want to thank the collectors who believed in my evolving work, especially those who allow the art to grow with them." She displayed the evolution history of each piece. When "The Whispering Face" appeared, people admired how uniquely it had transformed. Noah realized then that his interactions—every decision, every moment—had shaped the art.

He understood something at that moment: marketplaces weren't just places to buy things. They were ecosystems where stories, value, emotion, and identity came together. Each NFT carried history. Each auction carried drama. Each purchase carried meaning. And each collector carried responsibility. Noah walked out of the gallery with a new appreciation—not just for the art he owned, but for the world he had stepped into. The bidding room had changed him. It taught him that value wasn't only in rarity or price—it was in connection.

"The Whispering Facc" still evolves in his wallet to this day. And whenever it changes, Noah remembers the night he learned that digital marketplaces weren't about transactions. They were about transformation—both for the art and for the one who owned it.

Chapter 7

NFT Security, Storage & Protection

NFTs represent true digital ownership, but with true ownership comes true responsibility. Unlike traditional online accounts—where you can reset your password, recover access through customer support, or rely on a centralized entity to hold your assets—NFTs place the responsibility of security entirely on the user. There is no recovery button if you lose your private key. No phone number to call if someone drains your wallet. No company to reverse a fraudulent transaction. Once an NFT is transferred, burned, or stolen, the transaction is final. Understanding security, therefore, is not optional; it is the foundation upon which every NFT collector, creator, and investor must build. This chapter explores the essential protocols, best practices, and threat awareness required to protect your assets in the decentralized world of Web3.

At the core of NFT security is the **private key**. Your private key—represented as a string of cryptographic characters or a seed phrase of 12–24 words—is the master access key to your wallet. Anyone who gains access to your seed phrase effectively becomes you in the blockchain world. They can transfer your NFTs, send your crypto, execute smart contract interactions, and drain your entire digital identity within seconds. This is why your seed phrase must never be stored digitally in plain text, never typed into unknown websites, and never shared with any individual, platform, or supposed "support representative." Seed phrase scams are the No. 1 cause of NFT theft. The golden rule is simple: **if someone else has your seed phrase, you no longer own your assets.**

To strengthen your security, you must understand the difference between **hot wallets** and **cold wallets**. Hot wallets—such as MetaMask, Phantom, or Rainbow—are connected to the internet, making them convenient for daily use, minting, and interacting with marketplaces. However, this also means they are more vulnerable to phishing, hacks, malicious sites, and accidental transaction approvals. Cold wallets, also known as hardware wallets—such as Ledger or Trezor—store your private keys offline, making them nearly impossible to hack digitally. The best security practice for NFT holders is to use a combination of both: a hot wallet for browsing and minting, and a cold wallet for long-term storage of valuable NFTs. Transferring high-value assets to a hardware wallet dramatically reduces the risk of theft.

Another cornerstone of NFT security is **smart contract safety**. When you connect your wallet to a website or dApp, you are granting permissions to a smart contract. Some permissions are harmless—such as reading your wallet balance—but others can be dangerous, such as approval to transfer tokens on your behalf. Many users unknowingly sign malicious contract approvals, allowing scammers to drain assets without further confirmations. Always inspect transactions before signing. Avoid marketplaces, minting sites, Discord links, or Twitter links that are unverified. Use tools such as Etherscan Token Approvals, Revoke.cash, or Phantom's revoke feature to regularly check and remove unnecessary permissions from your wallet. Never approve unlimited spending permissions for unknown contracts. Understanding contract approvals is essential for avoiding invisible security traps.

The next layer of protection involves **phishing awareness**. Phishing attacks in Web3 are sophisticated. Scammers impersonate staff in Discord servers, steal verified Twitter accounts, create fake minting announcements, send hacked DMs, and produce forged websites that look identical to real ones. These scams attempt to trick users into entering seed phrases, approving malicious transactions, or connecting wallets to fake sites. To avoid these attacks, you must treat every link as suspicious until verified. Bookmark official project websites, avoid clicking mint links from DMs, disable direct messages on Discord, and verify that announcements come from official project channels. Assume that 90% of "urgent" messages online are scams designed to exploit fear or excitement.

Another key concept is **storage integrity**. Because NFTs reference off-chain metadata and asset files, you must ensure that the project uses decentralized storage solutions like IPFS, Arweave, or Filecoin. Centralized storage means a project's artwork, metadata, or entire collection could disappear if the server goes offline. Projects with on-chain or IPFS asset storage offer far greater long-term safety. Understanding where your NFT's assets are stored helps you evaluate the durability and legitimacy of any collection you buy.

You must also understand **transaction verification**. Every NFT transaction—minting, buying, selling, transferring—should be double-checked on a blockchain explorer such as Etherscan, Solscan, or Polygonscan. Verifying transactions allows you to detect suspicious activity, confirm authenticity, and ensure that contracts are legitimate. If you are minting a new NFT, verify the smart contract address through multiple official sources before proceeding. If a deal looks too good to be true, it usually is.

A final layer of protection involves **wallet segmentation and operational hygiene**. Never use the same wallet to mint risky projects and store high-value assets. Use different wallets for minting, trading, staking, and holding. Back up your seed phrase in multiple secure physical locations. Enable two-factor authentication on all exchange accounts. Keep software updated. Treat your digital assets with the same seriousness as a physical safe containing cash, jewelry, or legal documents. The decentralized world rewards users who adopt strong operational habits.

NFT security is not about paranoia—it is about empowerment. Once you understand how threats operate and how to protect yourself, the Web3 ecosystem becomes a place of freedom rather than fear. You control your assets. You control your identity. You control your future. With the right security mindset, your NFTs become not just valuable investments, but safe and resilient digital property in a world built on trustless technology. Mastering these principles ensures that everything you own today remains yours tomorrow.

"The Wallet With Two Keys"

Alina Shaw had always been careful. She double-checked door locks, memorized her passwords, and backed up her computer files twice. Her friends teased her about it, but she didn't mind. Being careful made her feel safe. So when she entered the world of NFTs, she assumed her natural habits would protect her. For a while, they did. She collected several beautiful pieces—digital paintings, animated portraits, and even a rare generative artwork she adored. Her collection became her sanctuary, a personal museum stored inside a glowing wallet icon on her screen. She felt confident, prepared, and secure...until the night everything changed.

It happened when she received a message from someone claiming to be an admin from a project she followed. The message looked official. The profile picture matched. The server badge matched. The tone felt professional. "We're issuing a contract update," the message said. "Please verify your wallet to avoid losing access." Alina hesitated. Something about it felt slightly off. But fear crept into her mind—*What if it was real? What if she ignored it and lost her NFTs?* Against her better judgment, she clicked the link.

The website looked identical to the project's real site—same colors, same layout, same branding. She connected her wallet. A transaction popped up. It wasn't asking to transfer funds or NFTs. It simply requested "permission to access tokens." It looked harmless. She approved it. Nothing happened. The site didn't update. She refreshed the page, confused. Moments later, she received a new notification—one that sent a chill down her spine. *Two of her NFTs were gone*. Transferred. Not by her. She checked the blockchain explorer. The tokens were now in another wallet. Panic ripped through her chest. Her hands trembled. She felt sick. She had been scammed. For hours she stared at her screen, unable to move, replaying the moment she clicked the link. She couldn't believe she had fallen for it—*she* who was always so careful, so cautious. Her heart ached not just for the financial loss, but for the emotional bond she had developed with her NFTs. They weren't just tokens—they were pieces of her story. She cried that night, overwhelmed by shame and regret. She vowed never to open her wallet again. But the next morning, something inside her refused to let the story end in defeat.

She joined security-focused Discord groups. She watched livestreams from cybersecurity experts. She learned about smart contract approvals, wallet permissions, revoking access, hardware wallets, phishing signatures, multisig protection, and IPFS integrity. She learned how scammers operated—not with magic, but with deception, mimicry, and timing. She began to understand her mistake wasn't carelessness. It was trust in a world where everything must be questioned.

Weeks later, she bought a hardware wallet. When she held it in her hand, it felt heavier than she expected—not physically, but symbolically. She set it up, transferred her remaining NFTs into it, and secured her seed phrase in multiple hidden places only she knew. With each step, she felt herself regaining control. Her confidence returned, stronger and wiser than before.

One day, she attended a virtual meetup where the speaker—a well-known collector—discussed NFT safety. When the Q&A opened, Alina hesitated before sharing her story. Her voice trembled as she told the audience how she lost her NFTs. She expected judgment. Instead, she received understanding. People told her their own stories—hack attempts, mistakes, losses—from newcomers to veterans. She realized she wasn't alone. She wasn't foolish. She was human in a new world full of hidden dangers.

After the event, several members messaged her privately. They thanked her for speaking up. Her story helped them tighten their own security. Her mistake had protected others. That thought filled her with a pride she didn't expect. She kept learning. She taught others. She became known among her community as someone who could spot phishing links instantly, who could explain contract permissions simply, who could calm newcomers when they felt overwhelmed.

Months later, she purchased a new NFT—a small, beautifully drawn illustration of a golden key. She named it *"Second Chance."* It wasn't expensive. It wasn't rare. But it meant everything to her. She stored it safely in her hardware wallet—a symbol of loss, recovery, wisdom, and strength. Her collection grew again, this time protected by layers of security she understood deeply. She had lost two NFTs, but she had gained something far more valuable: confidence backed by knowledge. Alina Shaw never fell for another scam again. And whenever she met someone new entering the NFT world, she always offered the same advice: "Protect your wallet like it holds something priceless—because one day, it will."

Chapter 8

NFT Communities, Culture & Collaboration

NFTs are not just digital assets—they are social assets. Their value is deeply connected to the communities surrounding them. The most successful NFT collections in history did not rise in price solely because of rarity or artwork. They rose because they built culture, identity, belonging, and momentum. In Web3, the saying "community is utility" is not just a slogan; it is an economic truth. If an NFT collection builds a thriving community, it can sustain long-term value even when the market fluctuates. If a project neglects community, even the strongest roadmap or artwork can collapse. Understanding NFT communities and culture is essential for evaluating collections, participating in Web3 socially, and building your own projects with a loyal base of supporters.

NFT communities typically form across multiple platforms: Discord, Twitter (X), Telegram, Farcaster, Lens, and in some cases dedicated websites or metaverse spaces. Discord is the heart of most NFT communities—it is where holders gather, where announcements are made, where collaborations form, where support is given, and where culture emerges naturally.

Successful communities use Discord not just as a chatroom but as a digital home. They organize channels for updates, art sharing, fan creations, trading discussions, tutorials, governance votes, and social hangouts. Moderators play a crucial role in keeping the community safe, engaged, and aligned with the project's values. A strong Discord feels alive, helpful, welcoming, and active. A failing Discord feels empty, hostile, chaotic, or full of bots.

Culture emerges from repeated interactions, shared humor, rituals, and common purpose. Some NFT cultures revolve around memes, inside jokes, and playful identity. Others revolve around serious art appreciation, tech innovation, education, or financial strategy. Some communities build lore—fictional universes, characters, and narratives that connect members emotionally. Others focus on collective growth, mental health, entrepreneurship, gaming, or philanthropy. The culture around an NFT project becomes its "soul." It is what draws new people in and keeps old members loyal. Culture cannot be faked—it must emerge authentically through shared experiences.

Another major dimension of NFT communities is **collaboration**. Unlike traditional brands that compete independently, Web3 encourages projects to collaborate, share visibility, cross-pollinate audiences, and co-create value.

Collaborations may involve joint art drops, co-branded NFTs, shared utility, metaverse events, combined storytelling, or reciprocal benefits for holders. These collaborations expand reach and strengthen trust. Collections that collaborate often appear more active, innovative, and interconnected. A strong collaboration strategy also makes holders feel like their NFTs give them access to a network of opportunities beyond one single project.

Beyond collaboration, many communities practice **co-creation**, where holders influence the direction of the project, propose ideas, vote on decisions, help design traits, contribute artwork, or create content. This transforms holders from passive investors into active participants. Co-creation builds ownership, loyalty, and pride. For example, some PFP communities allow holders to use their NFTs as characters in comics, animations, or stories. Others allow holders to form clubs, IRL meetups, or sub-communities within the main ecosystem. When holders feel they are shaping the project, the bond deepens dramatically.

A critical concept in community dynamics is **social capital**. In Web3, your reputation is linked to your activities, contributions, and wallet holdings. Early supporters of major projects often gain influence in the ecosystem. People build entire identities around their NFT PFPs, using them on social platforms, in business meetings, in virtual worlds, and even on resumes. Holding certain NFTs can grant you status, credibility, and opportunities in the Web3 space. Communities with strong social capital tend to attract founders, creators, entrepreneurs, and passionate supporters who shape the culture organically.

For project creators, building a healthy NFT community requires consistency, transparency, communication, and empathy. Silence from the founding team destroys trust quickly. Overpromising and underdelivering leads to frustration. Treating the community as investors instead of partners creates division. The best NFT communities operate with honesty, frequent updates, realistic expectations, and attention to the emotional temperature of holders. Leaders who show their faces, join voice chats, answer questions, and acknowledge mistakes build legendary communities that last.

From a collector's perspective, evaluating community health is essential before buying. Look for signs of genuine engagement: real conversations, meaningful interactions, educational value, creative sharing, and organic enthusiasm. Avoid communities full of spam, hype messages, price obsession, or hostility. Healthy communities talk about more than "floor price." They talk about art, identity, creativity, storytelling, and shared goals. These communities often outperform financially because holders are aligned emotionally, not just monetarily. Finally, NFT communities influence the broader culture of Web3. They push boundaries in digital identity, creativity, governance, and collaboration. They create trends, shape narratives, and evolve the ecosystem. The communities are the builders. The innovators. The storytellers. When you understand how these communities function, you gain insight into the heart of Web3 itself. In this chapter, you learn that NFTs are more than tokens—they are social revolutions, powered by people.

"The Room That Welcomed Her"

When Serena Cho bought her first NFT, she did it quietly. She didn't tell her friends, who already thought her tech interests were eccentric. She didn't announce it online. She simply clicked the "buy" button on a piece she loved—a pastel-colored character with soft eyes and a gentle smile. She didn't know much about NFT communities at the time. She thought she was just buying a digital artwork. She had no idea she was about to enter a new world.

After her purchase, she noticed a link in the description: "Join our Discord." She hesitated. Discord was something she associated with gamers, not art collectors. But curiosity nudged her forward. She clicked the link and entered a server named "DreamSprouts." At first, she felt overwhelmed.

Messages filled the screen. People were sharing art. Joking. Supporting each other. Talking about events. She lingered silently, observing. She felt like an outsider in a room where everyone seemed to know one another.

But everything changed when someone noticed her new member tag and typed, "Welcome, Serena! Show us your Sprout!" Others chimed in with emojis and greetings. Serena froze for a moment. Then she posted her NFT. The response shocked her. People celebrated her choice. "That one is beautiful!" "Great pick!" "The colors on yours are rare!" She felt warmth spreading in her chest. For the first time in a long time, strangers made her feel seen.

Over the next days, she learned what DreamSprouts really was—a global community of artists, collectors, developers, teachers, and dreamers. They hosted weekly voice chats where people talked about creativity, life, and goals. They ran art contests, shared tips for digital painting, and even organized mental health check-ins. Serena joined a drawing challenge one evening, expecting no one to notice her submission. To her surprise, dozens of members commented, encouraging her to keep creating.

One night, she joined a "Lore Session," where the founders revealed new parts of the DreamSprouts universe. The story was whimsical, magical, and emotional—each character represented different aspects of hope. Serena listened intently, captivated. The artists asked the community for suggestions on future story arcs. Serena hesitated, then typed an idea about a character that healed others with music. The founder read it aloud. "That's beautiful," he said. "Let's explore that." Her heart raced. They valued her voice.

Weeks turned into months. Serena found herself logging into the server each night not out of obligation, but out of joy. She made friends in different countries. She attended virtual events. She collaborated on a fan-made comic. She even helped newcomers find their way, remembering how nervous she had been her first day. The once-intimidating chatroom had become a home.

But the most transformative moment came one evening during a community town hall. The founders discussed expanding DreamSprouts into a metaverse space and asked for volunteers to help. Serena felt a spark—she had always dreamed of working in digital art. She raised her hand, offering to assist with concept sketches. To her astonishment, they welcomed her immediately. "Your style fits perfectly with our vision," they said.

Working with the team changed everything. Serena felt her

confidence grow as she collaborated on character designs, story elements, and world-building concepts. Her contributions were celebrated publicly. Her art was even featured in a DreamSprouts exhibition event in a virtual gallery. When she saw her artwork displayed on glowing walls surrounded by avatars admiring it, tears filled her eyes. She had never experienced something so validating.

One night, she sat quietly at her desk, looking at her DreamSprout NFT glowing on her screen. She whispered, "You brought me here." She realized that the art she bought months earlier wasn't just a purchase—it was a key. A door. A connection to a world where she felt understood. The community didn't just support her art—they supported her growth, her courage, her identity.

Serena often told newcomers the same thing: "You think you're buying art. But really, you're finding your people."

And for her, that made all the difference.

Chapter 9

NFT Art, Design & Creator Economy

NFTs have transformed the creator economy by giving artists, designers, musicians, filmmakers, writers, and innovators something the digital world never provided before: **true ownership, global distribution, programmable royalties, and direct-to-collector relationships**. In the traditional art world, creators rely on galleries, agents, publishers, or platforms that take significant cuts of revenue and control much of the exposure. In social media ecosystems, creators receive likes and followers but often struggle to monetize their work sustainably. NFTs solve these structural barriers by giving creators full control over their distribution, pricing, brand, and long-term revenue. Understanding NFT art, design theory, collection structure, and the creator economy is essential for anyone entering Web3 as an artist or creator.

At the heart of NFT art is **digital expression**. Artists are no longer confined to physical canvas or traditional mediums. They experiment with animation, 3D modeling, generative systems, AI-assisted art, soundscapes, programmable visuals, interactive pieces, and dynamically evolving artworks. The blockchain enables these digital formats to be collectible and ownable. NFT art is not simply "art placed on a blockchain." It is a new category of artistic creation unique to the digital-native era. Generative art, for example, uses code to produce algorithmic patterns, colors, or structures that are minted as unique outputs. Each variation is distinct, and randomness becomes part of the creative process. AI art blends human prompting with machine interpretation. Interactive NFTs change based on user actions. Dynamic NFTs evolve over time. All these forms redefine what "digital art" means.

Designing NFT collections requires an understanding of **visual identity, composition, style consistency, and rarity distribution**. For one-of-one artists, each piece may be unique and independent. For 10K PFP collections or themed batches, the design must maintain coherence across thousands of variations. This requires clearly defined traits—backgrounds, accessories, expressions, themes, textures, color palettes, and stylistic rules. Consistency is essential because collectors evaluate the visual cohesion of the entire collection. Rarity design determines which traits appear frequently and which are reserved for the most valuable pieces. Designers strategically distribute rare attributes to create excitement, prestige, and collectibility. Well-designed rarity systems often lead to strong market performance and enhance the artistic core of the project. Beyond design, creators must understand **storytelling and lore**, which increasingly influence the success of NFT art. Many collections incorporate worldbuilding narratives that explain the characters, their origins, their missions, and their relationships. Lore enriches the artistic experience and gives collectors emotional connection and identity. Story-driven collections form passionate communities and become intellectual properties that expand into comics, animations, games, novels, merchandise, and metaverse experiences. The best NFT collections mix art with narrative and evolve their universe over time through updates, events, collaborations, or seasonal drops.

NFTs also change how creators earn money. The **economics of NFTs** allow creators to monetize upfront through primary sales and continuously through royalties on secondary sales. A single artwork may generate revenue for years as collectors trade it. This incentivizes creators to build long-term brands rather than depend solely on one-time commissions. It rewards authenticity, consistency, and community presence. NFT artists often become entrepreneurs: managing their brand, communicating with collectors, planning drops, building email lists, hosting virtual exhibitions, and collaborating with other creators. The Web3 creator is not just an artist—they are a business entity with global reach.

Another key aspect of the creator economy is **direct-to-community interaction**. Collectors are no longer faceless buyers. They become supporters, collaborators, promoters, and evangelists. Artists forge relationships with their collectors through Discord servers, livestreams, Twitter (X) spaces, digital meetups, and behind-the-scenes content. Collectors appreciate transparency, authenticity, and dedication. Some collectors even become patrons, buying multiple pieces from the same artist and championing their career. This dynamic mirrors historical artist–patron relationships but on a decentralized, global scale. NFT spaces reward artists who engage thoughtfully and build trust.

Creators must also understand **pricing strategies**. Pricing NFT art is a delicate balance between accessibility and perceived value. Too high, and collectors ignore it. Too low, and the art is undervalued or seen as amateur. Successful pricing strategies depend on the artist's reputation, the uniqueness of the art, quality of execution, community presence, and the emotional resonance of the work. Many creators begin with affordable editions to build a collector base, then gradually raise prices as demand grows. Others launch limited high-end pieces that establish prestige. Whatever the strategy, consistency and clarity matter.

Creators entering Web3 must also master **platform selection**. One-of-one artists often choose Foundation, SuperRare, or Exchange Art. PFP creators lean toward OpenSea, Magic Eden, or custom contract minting sites. Photographers gravitate toward platforms like Quantum or Ethblockart. Musicians explore Sound.xyz or Royal. Each platform caters to specific audiences and artistic cultures, and choosing the right home is essential for visibility and brand positioning.

Finally, Web3 creators must embrace **long-term brand building**. NFT success rarely happens overnight. The market rewards artists who are consistent, who evolve their craft, who nurture their communities, and who explore creative frontiers. Artistic integrity matters more in Web3 than in any other digital medium. The artists who endure are those who remain true to their vision while adapting to new technologies and opportunities.

NFTs are not only transforming digital art—they are transforming creators themselves. They are giving artists financial independence, global exposure, and unprecedented empowerment. The future of creation is decentralized, collaborative, and borderless, and those who understand the NFT creator economy will shape the next generation of digital culture.

"The Artist Who Painted With Code"

Mina Alvarez had always painted the same way—brush in hand, canvas on easel, quiet music in the background. Her artwork was soft, emotional, and deeply human. But as the world changed, she felt left behind. Galleries rejected her applications. Social media buried her posts. Commissions paid little. She worked part-time at a coffee shop to cover rent, wondering if her dream would ever become possible. She felt invisible, unheard, and tired. One evening, while scrolling through her phone, she stumbled across a video titled: *"NFTs Are Changing Art Forever."* She almost ignored it—but something inside her clicked. She opened it.

The video showed artists using animation, generative algorithms, 3D rendering, and dynamic data to create art that evolved, responded, and lived on the blockchain. Mina's eyes widened. She never imagined art could exist that way. She spent the entire night down a rabbit hole of digital galleries, virtual exhibitions, and NFT marketplaces filled with art unlike anything she had ever seen. She wasn't intimidated. She was inspired. For the first time in months, she felt that familiar spark of creation rising inside her.

Over the next week, she learned about digital art tools—Photoshop, Procreate, Blender, and then something unexpected: generative art coded with JavaScript and

Processing. The idea terrified her. She had never written a line of code in her life. But when she watched a tutorial of a simple generative pattern shifting based on mathematical rules, she felt something shift inside her. What if code could become her new brush? What if she could paint with logic instead of pigment?

She practiced every night after her shift. She combined hand-painted textures with code-driven animation. She layered watercolor strokes with algorithmic movement. Her experiments were messy at first—glitchy shapes, awkward transitions, strange color shifts. But the more she learned, the more the artwork came alive. Her pieces began to breathe, expand, contract, shimmer, and pulse with life. It felt like discovering a new language of expression. She called her emerging style "organic generative."

When she minted her first NFT—a swirling, emotional piece called *"Heartbeat in Motion"*—she felt like she was stepping into a new chapter of her life. She didn't expect sales. She didn't expect followers. She just wanted to belong somewhere. But the next morning, she woke to a message: someone had bought it. The buyer wrote: "Your art feels human in a digital world." Tears streamed down Mina's face. That was exactly what she wanted her art to be.

As she released more pieces, her small collector base grew. They left encouraging messages, tagged her on social media, and even created animated fan edits of her work. One collector sent her a DM: "Your generative pieces remind me of emotions I can't describe." Another said, "Thank you for bringing softness to Web3." Mina realized then that her art wasn't just being purchased—it was being felt.

Months passed. Her technique evolved. Her income grew. She left her coffee shop job. She joined Twitter Spaces where artists shared their journeys, fears, and breakthroughs. She collaborated on a cross-chain collection that merged generative art with poetry. She participated in a virtual gallery show where her pieces floated inside a moonlit digital garden. People walked through the space as avatars, pausing in front of her work, admiring the blend of paint and code. Mina watched silently, heart full, as strangers connected with her art in ways she always dreamed possible.

One day, she received an invitation from a major NFT art platform: "We'd like to feature you as a spotlight artist." She froze. Her hands trembled. She had gone from a rejected gallery hopeful to a recognized creator in a global digital movement. When the feature launched, she saw her artwork on the platform's front page—glowing, breathing, beautiful. Collectors praised her innovation, her softness, her authenticity. She felt understood for the first time. Late one night, after finishing a new generative piece that flowed like liquid starlight, she looked at her screen and whispered, "I found my world." She realized that NFTs didn't just change her career—they changed her identity. She wasn't just an artist anymore. She was a digital storyteller. A coder of emotions. A creator in a borderless universe.

Her journey became a message she shared often: "Your art can evolve. You can evolve. And somewhere in the digital world, someone is waiting for the version of you that you're afraid to explore."

And that was the moment she understood: she didn't just paint with brushes anymore. **She painted with possibility.**

Chapter 10

The Future Of NFTs & Web3 Innovation

The NFT space has already transformed digital ownership, creativity, and online communities—but we are still at the very beginning of its evolution. NFTs are not a trend, nor a passing phase; they are the digital foundation for Web3's future. To understand where NFTs are going, you must grasp how technology, culture, business, finance, identity, and governance will converge in the coming decade. The future of NFTs lies in mass adoption, utility-driven design, real-world integration, regulatory clarity, interoperable ecosystems, AI collaboration, and widespread tokenization of assets across both digital and physical worlds. As NFTs mature, their role will expand far beyond art and collectibles. They will become the infrastructure for digital economies—and those who understand this shift will lead the next generation of innovation.

The first major transformation in NFTs is **real-world asset tokenization (RWA)**. Real estate, vehicles, businesses, intellectual property, luxury goods, stocks, commodities, and legal documents will be tokenized as NFTs to simplify ownership transfer, reduce fraud, and increase global liquidity. Instead of dealing with paperwork, middlemen, or regional limitations, an NFT representing a home deed or business share can transfer ownership instantly. Countries and major financial institutions are already experimenting with blockchain-based property records. The shift to tokenized ownership will unlock trillions of dollars in global assets, and NFTs will be the technological backbone of this transformation.

The second major evolution involves **identity and credentials**. Digital identity systems will rely on NFTs to store identity proofs, certifications, medical records, educational achievements, licenses, memberships, work history, and digital reputation—all in a secure, private, portable format. Instead of relying on passwords or centralized databases vulnerable to hacking, people will authenticate using cryptographic proofs tied to their wallets. These identity NFTs will not be publicly visible; they will be encrypted with zero-knowledge proofs, giving individuals control over what they reveal. This marks a shift toward self-sovereign identity, where individuals—not corporations—control their data.

Another pivotal future development is **NFT-based governance and DAOs**. Decentralized autonomous organizations use NFTs and tokens as voting tools, membership identifiers, and contribution badges. As DAOs mature, they will govern businesses, investment funds, entertainment franchises, metaverse cities, and even real-world communities. Members will vote on decisions, propose ideas, contribute resources, and shape the direction of decentralized entities. NFTs will function as governance passes that evolve based on participation, enabling more democratic, transparent, and collaborative systems of organization.

In parallel, NFTs will revolutionize **entertainment, gaming, and media**. Characters, items, skins, music, videos, tools, and game assets will exist across multiple platforms through interoperability. Imagine owning a single digital avatar that moves seamlessly across metaverse worlds, games, virtual conferences, and social platforms—customizable, monetizable, and fully portable. Studios will release films with NFT-based ticketing, fan perks, collectible scenes, behind-the-scenes passes, and interactive storytelling experiences. Musicians will release NFT albums with royalty-sharing mechanisms, private concerts, and token-gated communities. These innovations will blur the lines between creators and audiences.

One of the most powerful future shifts will come from the integration of **AI and NFTs**. AI-generated art, dynamic NFTs that learn from user behavior, evolving characters controlled by neural networks, and AI companions that live in the blockchain ecosystem will become mainstream. NFTs will serve as “vessels” for AI agents—digital assistants, mentors, or companions that users own and personalize. This fusion of artificial intelligence and blockchain ownership will open unprecedented creative and economic opportunities, forming a new category: **AI-native NFTs** capable of interacting, adapting, and growing.

We will also see the rise of **NFT-based brands and global IP ecosystems**. PFP collections will evolve into entertainment franchises, comic book worlds, gaming studios, fashion labels, and real-life consumer brands. This has already begun with successful collections forming partnerships with major companies, releasing merchandise, and developing animated series. The next generation will take this further—expanding their universes into metaverse theme parks, interoperable experiences, and cross-chain narratives that develop over years.

Regulation is another crucial component of the future. As governments understand NFTs better, regulatory clarity will emerge. This will attract institutional investors, large brands, and traditional financial institutions into the NFT ecosystem. Proper regulation will reduce scams, increase consumer confidence, and create standards that support mass adoption. NFTs tied to financial assets will require compliance, while purely creative NFTs will remain open and decentralized. This healthy separation will form the future legal framework for the space.

Perhaps the most important future trend is **user experience transformation**. Today, NFTs are complex for the average person. Wallets, seed phrases, gas fees, smart contracts—these concepts intimidate newcomers. The future will remove this complexity. Wallets will function like simple apps. Transactions will be gasless or invisible. Onboarding will take seconds. People will own NFTs without knowing they are using blockchain technology. This invisible integration will trigger the true mass adoption of Web3 and the final transition from Web2 platforms to Web3 ecosystems.

The future of NFTs is expansive, disruptive, and inevitable. It involves every industry, every country, every creative field, and every form of digital life. NFTs will unlock new careers, new businesses, new economies, and new cultural movements. Those who position themselves today will be pioneers tomorrow. This chapter reveals a simple truth: NFTs are not about pictures—they are about the architecture of the future internet. And that future belongs to the creators, builders, and visionaries who embrace it now.

"The World Inside The Glass City"

Adrian Hale had always dreamed of the future. As a child, he imagined floating cities, holographic gardens, and glowing skylines powered by impossible technology. But as he grew older, he watched the real world fall into routine—emails, commutes, deadlines. His imagination faded into the background. That changed the day he visited the Glass City.

It wasn't a physical place. It existed inside a metaverse world known as Solaris. Adrian had joined Solaris out of curiosity, but nothing prepared him for what he found. When he entered the portal, he emerged into a vast, shimmering city made entirely of transparent crystalline structures that refracted neon light across every surface. Buildings floated. Pathways curved like rivers of glass. Avatars glided effortlessly. And everything—every object, every sign, every structure—was powered by NFTs.

A guide avatar greeted him. "Welcome to the Glass City," she said. "Here, NFTs are not collectibles. They are the operating system of our world."

At first, Adrian didn't understand. But as he walked the streets, he saw the future in motion. Citizens showed identity badges stored as encrypted NFTs. Businesses accepted NFT-based licenses to operate. Homes were purchased by transferring NFT property deeds. A musician performed on a floating stage, and fans scanned their NFT concert passes for access. A chef streamed a cooking class where only holders of a special recipe NFT could join. Everywhere he turned, the blockchain pulsed beneath the city like a heartbeat.

Adrian followed the guide to a tall tower called the Registry Spire. Inside, holographic screens displayed maps of the city's activity. He saw datasets showing tokenized real estate sales, decentralized governance votes, upgrades to public spaces, and AI-powered NFT companions assisting users. "This is what happens when identity, ownership, and interaction merge," the guide said. "Web3 isn't a technology. It's an ecosystem."

As he explored deeper, he entered a district called The Living Market. Here, NFTs were not static images—they were alive. He saw an AI-powered pet NFT that learned from its owner. A dynamic garden NFT that changed with the seasons. A poem NFT that rewrote itself based on the holder's emotions. An avatar NFT that adapted its appearance according to the wearer's digital journey. Adrian felt wonder blooming inside him. He had never seen technology so human.

In a quiet corner of the market stood an old man sculpting light. With a wave of his hand, he shaped beams into elegant forms. Adrian watched mesmerized. "What are you creating?"

he asked. The old man smiled. "Stories," he said. As the sculpture crystallized, Adrian realized it was an NFT—one that recorded the conversation they had just shared. It stored memory, emotion, and interaction. "In Web3," the man said, "art is no longer created once. It continues writing itself as you live."

As night fell across the Glass City, the skyline erupted in luminous blues and purples. Adrian stood on a balcony overlooking the metropolis. He felt something stirring in him—something he had lost years ago. Imagination. Possibility. Hope. The guide joined him quietly. "You understand now, don't you?" she said. "NFTs aren't pictures. They're architecture. They are the connective tissue of the future."

Adrian nodded slowly. "This world... it's what I always dreamed the future would be."

"It can be," she said. "In time, the physical world will look like this too. The transition has already begun. You can help shape it."

A single question formed in his mind: *How?*

The guide extended her hand, and a glowing NFT appeared—shaped like a seed made of light. "This is your key to Solaris," she said. "A builder's token. With it, you can create, collaborate, and write your part of the story. Web3 is not waiting for permission. It is waiting for creators."

Adrian held the seed in his palm. It pulsed gently like a heartbeat. And in that moment, he felt the spark he had lost as a child ignite once more. The future wasn't something to watch—it was something to build.

He looked out at the Glass City—alive, evolving, radiant—and whispered, "I'm ready."

And somewhere deep within the metaverse, the city whispered back: "Welcome home, builder."

Epilogue

The world of NFTs is still young, still growing, and still defining itself. When you first opened this book, you may have thought NFTs were simply images, collectibles, or speculative assets traded by early adopters online. But as you journeyed through each chapter, you discovered something much deeper. NFTs are not just a new form of digital art—they represent a fundamental shift in how humans create, own, trade, express identity, collaborate, and participate in the digital economy. They are a bridge between technology and creativity, between code and culture, between imagination and value. And most importantly, they are the building blocks of Web3's future. This epilogue is a moment of reflection—not on what NFTs have been, but on what they can become through people like you.

The essence of NFTs lies in **ownership**, a concept that has shaped societies since the beginning of civilization. But for decades, the digital world lacked true ownership. Everything was infinitely copyable, centralized, fragile, and dependent on external platforms. NFTs changed that. They introduced digital scarcity, authenticity, and permanence. They gave creators economic power. They gave collectors a voice. They gave communities a home. They turned the internet into a place where digital objects can have real meaning, real emotion, and real value. This shift is not temporary—it is permanent. And it signals a new chapter in the evolution of human expression.

Throughout this book, you learned how NFTs empower creators through programmable royalties, global marketplaces, community-driven projects, and technology that eliminates gatekeepers. You learned how NFT buyers evaluate collections—examining rarity, culture, utility, and team credibility. You explored the importance of security, safe storage, and protecting your assets in a decentralized world. You saw how communities form, collaborate, share stories, build identities, and support creators in ways traditional industries never allowed. You discovered how NFTs are shaping the future of gaming, entertainment, work, and global ownership. And in every chapter, you saw that NFTs are not static—they are alive, evolving alongside the technology and people who shape them.

As we stand at the edge of Web3's next leap, NFTs remain at the center of innovation. AI-powered NFTs will become interactive companions. Dynamic NFTs will evolve based on user behavior or real-world data. Tokenized real-world assets will transform how people buy homes, register businesses, secure loans, access health records, and authenticate identities. Digital fashion will merge with physical fashion. Metaverse identities will influence real-world reputations. Decentralized communities will build businesses, brands, and intellectual property. And creators will grow into global entrepreneurs without asking for permission from middlemen. This is not science fiction. This is a roadmap quietly unfolding across the world.

But the most important lesson is this: **NFTs gain meaning from the people who believe in them.** Technology alone cannot create culture. Code cannot build trust. Blockchains cannot generate passion. It is humans—artists, collectors, dreamers, builders, investors, storytellers—who breathe life into NFTs. The technology may be new, but the motivations behind it are timeless: connection, expression, identity, belonging, and the pursuit of possibility. NFTs succeed because people see themselves in them. They become mirrors of creativity, symbols of status, or badges of community. They become memories, milestones, and legacies. They become stories worth telling.

You are now part of that story. Whether you create NFTs, collect them, analyze them, or simply appreciate them, your presence shapes the space. Every decision you make—every mint, purchase, collaboration, conversation, or idea—ripples across the ecosystem. Your choices influence artists, communities, markets, and futures. And as more people enter this space, they will look to pioneers like you to understand what is possible. You are early, but being early means more than timing. It means responsibility. It means opportunity. It means potential. And it means you have the chance to lead.

So as this book concludes, consider this your invitation. Not just to participate, but to build. Not just to observe, but to innovate. The next era of NFTs will not be created by corporations alone. It will be shaped by individuals who dare to imagine new formats, new worlds, and new definitions of value. The artists who experiment. The collectors who support them. The developers who push boundaries. The communities who uplift each other. And the visionaries who refuse to limit themselves to the past. In Web3, you are not just a user—you are a co-architect of the future.

And so, the journey continues. Beyond this book. Beyond the series. Beyond the horizon of what we currently understand. The future of NFTs is open, expansive, and waiting for the next wave of creators and innovators to leave their mark. You now possess the knowledge, tools, mindset, and confidence to step forward. You know the risks. You know the opportunities. You know the possibilities. Every great movement begins with a small group of people willing to dream. And now, you are one of them.

As you close this book, remember: **NFTs are not the end of something— they are the beginning.**

The beginning of new industries. New careers. New cultures. New economies. And new stories that the world has never seen before.

Your chapter is only just starting. Welcome to the future of ownership.

www.ingramcontent.com/pod-product-compliance
Lightning Source LLC
LaVergne TN
LVHW080531210926
848481LV00021B/2330
9798295491122